# Presented to

CAMERON

_____

 ## From

MOM

_____

 ## Date

10/23/96

_____

All Scripture quotations are from The King James Version of the Bible.

ISBN 1-55748-712-X

Barbour & Company, Inc., P.O. Box 719, Uhrichsville, Ohio 44683

The KJV Bible for Toddlers

Bible Stories for Toddlers from the Old and New Testaments

Randy Kryszewski

Illustrated by
Caren Jurina

A BARBOUR BOOK

Old Testament Contents

New Testament Contents

Heaven and Earth

In the beginning God created the heaven and the the earth. And the earth was without form . . . and darkness was upon the face of the deep . . . .   *Genesis 1:1-2*

God made the sky. God made the stars. God made the sun and the moon. The sun keeps us warm. The moon helps us see at night. God knew just what we needed.

And God said, Let the earth bring forth the living creature after his kind, cattle, and creeping thing, and beast of the earth of his kind: and it was so.   *Genesis 1:24*

God made every plant and tree. God made fish and birds. God made each and every kind of animal, too. Thank You, God, for making so many wonderful things.

Adam and Eve

And God said, "Let us make man in our image, after our likeness: and let them have dominion . . . over all of the earth . . . .   Genesis 1:26

God wanted someone to take care of all that He had made. So God made a man. God called the man Adam. God told Adam to take care of this wonderful new world.

So God created man in his own image, in the image of God created he him; male and female created he them.   *Genesis 1:27*

God also made a woman. God called the woman Eve. Eve was Adam's new friend. Adam and Eve were the very first man and woman. God loved Adam and Eve very much. God loves you, too.

A Beautiful Garden

And the Lord God planted a garden eastward in Eden; and there he put the man whom he had formed.
                                                                    Genesis 2:8

God planted a beautiful garden called Eden. The garden was filled with fruit trees. God told Adam and Eve to eat the fruit from any tree they wished, except from the tree in the middle of the garden.

But of the tree of knowledge of good and evil, thou shalt not eat of it: for in the day thou eatest thereof thou shalt surely die.   *Genesis 2:17*

God told Adam and Eve that the fruit from this tree would hurt them if they ate some. So Adam and Eve obeyed God and did not eat the fruit from this tree.

Adam and Eve Sin

And the Lord God called unto Adam, and said unto him, Where art thou? . . . Hast thou eaten of the tree . . . that thou shouldest not eat?   *Genesis 3:9-11*

One day a sneaky snake talked to Eve. He told Eve to disobey God and eat the special fruit. He said, "This fruit will make you just like God." Eve believed the snake and ate the special fruit.

Therefore the Lord God sent him forth from the garden of Eden, to till the ground from whence he was taken.   *Genesis 3:23*

Adam ate some of the fruit, also. Adam and Eve were very sad. They had disobeyed God. God made Adam and Eve leave the garden. God loved Adam and Eve. God still took care of them.

Noah Builds the Ark

And God said unto Noah, The end of all flesh is come before me . . . Make thee an ark of gopherwood . . . .   Genesis 6:13-14

Noah was a good man. Noah obeyed God. God loved Noah very much. God told Noah to build a big boat. So Noah obeyed God and built a big boat. God told Noah a great flood was coming.

And of every living thing of all flesh, two of every sort shalt thou bring into the ark, to keep them alive with thee; they shall be male and female.   *Genesis 6:19*

God told Noah to put many animals on the boat. Noah filled the boat with food for the animals. Noah put his family on the boat, too. When everyone was on the boat, God shut the door.

A Big Flood

And the rain was upon the earth forty days and forty nights . . . and the waters increased, and bare up the ark . . . above the earth.   *Genesis 7:12-17*

The great flood came, just as God had said. It rained for forty days and nights. Noah and his family were safe on the big boat. The animals were safe, too. Everything else on earth died.

And God blessed Noah and his sons, and said unto them, Be fruitful, and multiply, and replenish the earth . . . I establish my covenant with you . . . . *Genesis 9:1-9*

One day the rain stopped. The great flood was over. God told Noah to let the animals out of the boat. Noah and his family also came out of the boat. Noah thanked God for saving his family.

People Speak Differently

And the whole earth was of one language . . . and they said, Go to, let us build us a city and a tower, whose top may reach unto heaven.   *Genesis 11:1-4*

After the great flood, the earth was filled with people again. They decided to build a tall tower. They wanted to feel big. God saw the tall tower. God knew it was time for a change.

18

. . . The Lord said . . . they have all one language . . . let us go down, and there confound their language, that they may not understand one another's speech.   *Genesis 11:6-7*

So God made the people speak in many new ways. Now they could not talk to each other. They did not feel big anymore. So God moved them to many new places where people who talked alike could understand each other.

Abraham and Sarah

. . . And the Lord did unto Sarah as he had spoken. For Sarah conceived, and bare Abraham a son in his old age, at the set time . . . .   *Genesis 21:1-2*

Do you see Sarah? Sarah is very old. Sarah and her husband Abraham wanted a baby. Sarah could not have a baby. Sarah was too old to have a baby. Then God helped Sarah and Abraham.

And Abraham called the name of his son that was born unto him, whom Sarah bare to him, Isaac . . . Abraham was a hundred years old . . . .   *Genesis 21:3-5*

God helped Sarah to have a baby boy. Abraham was very happy. Abraham named the baby boy Isaac. Sarah and Abraham loved Isaac very much. Thank You, God, for helping Sarah.

Twins Are Born

And the Lord said unto her, Two nations are in thy womb . . . the one people shall be stronger than the other . . . and the elder shall serve the younger.   *Genesis 25:23*

God helped Rebekah to have two baby boys. The boys' names were Jacob and Esau. Rebekah loved Jacob very much. Jacob did not like to go outside. He liked to be near his mother.

And the boys grew: and Esau was a cunning hunter, a man of the field; and Jacob was a plain man, dwelling in tents.   *Genesis 25:27*

Esau was very strong. Esau liked to go outside. Esau was a very good hunter. Isaac is Esau's father. Isaac loved Esau very much. Isaac liked to eat the food that Esau made.

Jacob Makes a Trade

And Esau said to Jacob, Feed me, I pray thee, with that same red pottage; for I am faint . . . And Jacob said, Sell me this day thy birthright.   Genesis 25:30-31

One day, Esau had been outside a long time. Esau was very tired. Esau was also very hungry. When Esau got home, he saw Jacob cooking some food. The food smelled very good.

And Esau said, Behold, I am at the point to die: and what profit shall this birthright do to me . . . and he sold his birthright unto Jacob. *Genesis 25:32-33*

"Give me some food," said Esau. Jacob said, "I will give you some food if you give me something. Give me your birthday blessing, and I will give you some food." Esau gave Jacob his birthday blessing.

Jacob Gets a Blessing

And Rebekah spake unto Jacob . . . saying, Behold, I heard thy father speak unto Esau . . . only obey my voice . . . go now . . . fetch me . . . two good kids of the goats.

Genesis 27:6-9

Esau's father was going to give Esau a special blessing. Esau's mother wanted Jacob to get the special blessing. She told Jacob to trick his father and pretend to be Esau.

And Jacob said unto his father, I am Esau thy first-born . . . sit and eat of my venison, that thy soul may bless me. *Genesis 27:19*

So Jacob put on some of his brother's clothes. Jacob's mother cooked some food for Jacob to give to his father. Isaac thought that Jacob really was Esau and gave Jacob the special blessing.

God Speaks to Jacob

And he lighted upon a certain place, and tarried there all night . . . and he took . . . stones . . . and put them for his pillows, and lay down in that place to sleep.   Genesis 28:11

One day when Jacob was older he went for a walk. When it was nighttime, Jacob got very tired and went to sleep. And while Jacob was sleeping, he had a very special dream.

And he dreamed, and behold, a ladder set up on the earth, and . . . it reached to heaven: and behold, the angels of God ascending and descending on it. *Genesis 28:12*

In his dream, Jacob saw a ladder with angels walking on it. God was at the very top of this ladder. God spoke to Jacob and said, "I am the God of your father, I will give you this land."

Jacob Meets Rachel

And he looked, and behold, a well in the field . . . there were three flocks of sheep lying by it . . . and a great stone was upon the well's mouth. *Genesis 29:2*

Jacob went on a trip. Jacob stopped to rest near a well. There was a big stone on the top of the well. Jacob saw a beautiful woman coming to the well. Jacob moved the big stone on top of the well.

. . . Rachel came with her father's sheep: for she kept them . . . and Jacob kissed Rachel
. . . And Jacob loved Rachel.   *Genesis 29:9-18*

The beautiful woman was Rachel. Jacob moved the big stone so Rachel could give her sheep a drink of water. Rachel liked Jacob. He had been very nice to her. Jacob liked Rachel, too.

Joseph's Brothers Are Mad

Now Israel loved Joseph more than all his children, because he was the son of his old age: and he made him a coat of many colors. *Genesis 37:3*

Do you see Joseph's colorful coat? Joseph's father gave him a colorful coat because he loved Joseph. Joseph's brothers were mad. They wanted to hurt Joseph.

Come, and let us sell him to the Ishmeelites, and let not our hand be upon him . . . for he is our flesh. And his brethren were content.   *Genesis 37:27*

So the angry brothers sold Joseph as a slave to some men nearby. Joseph's father did not know where Joseph was. He was very sad because he loved Joseph very much. Joseph was sad, too.

God Helps Joseph

. . . Joseph was brought down to Egypt; and Potiphar, an officer of Pharaoh . . . bought him of the hands of the Ishmeelites . . . .   *Genesis 39:1*

Now Joseph was a slave. A man named Potiphar bought Joseph. He made Joseph do work for him. God helped Joseph do his work. Potiphar liked Joseph because he did very good work.

And the Lord was with Joseph, and he was a prosperous man . . . in the house of his master the Egyptian . . . Joseph found grace in his sight . . . .   Genesis 39:2-4

Potiphar put Joseph in charge of his whole house. Joseph was a very good man. Joseph knew that God was helping him. Joseph loved God. And God loved Joseph.

Joseph Helps His Brothers

. . . Behold I have heard that there is corn in Egypt: get you down thither, and buy for us from thence . . . and Joseph's ten brethren went down . . . to Egypt. Genesis 42:2-3

Joseph had many brothers. Joseph's brothers did not live in Egypt. They lived in Canaan, with their father. There was no food in Canaan. So Joseph's brothers went to Egypt to buy food.

And Joseph said unto his brethren, I am Joseph . . . your brother, whom ye sold into Egypt . . . for God did send me before you to preserve life.   *Genesis 45:3-5*

When Joseph's brothers got to Egypt, they did not know who Joseph was. When Joseph told them he was their brother, they were glad. Joseph gave them food. God helped Joseph and his family.

Israelites Become Slaves

Now there arose up a new king over Egypt . . . And he said . . . the children of Israel are . . . mightier than we . . . let us deal wisely with them . . . .   Exodus 1:8-10

The new Pharoah did not like the Israelites. He was afraid that one day they would be too strong. So the Israelites became slaves in Egypt.

Therefore they did set over them task-masters . . . And they built for Pharaoh treasure-cities . . . in mortar, and in brick . . . .   *Exodus 1:11-14*

The Israelites were forced to work hard at making bricks and huge buildings for Pharoah. This made the Israelites very sad.

Baby Moses Is Safe

. . . The woman conceived and bare a son . . . he was a goodly child . . . And when she could not longer hide him . . . she took . . . an ark . . . and she laid it . . . by the river's brink. *Exodus 2:2-3*

Pharaoh said, "No more Israelite baby boys!" Do you see baby Moses? He is an Israelite. His mother hid him here. Who will take care of baby Moses? Who will help him?

And the daughter of Pharaoh came down to wash herself at the river . . . she saw the child . . . she had compassion on him . . . .   *Exodus 2:5-6*

A princess found baby Moses. She is Pharaoh's daughter. The princess loved baby Moses. She will not tell anyone that baby Moses is an Israelite. She gave baby Moses a new home.

God Talks to Moses

. . . Moses kept the flock . . . And the Angel of the Lord appeared unto him in a flame of fire out of the midst of a bush . . . and, behold, the bush was not consumed.

Exodus 3:1-2

Moses is not a baby anymore. Moses is older now. One day Moses went for a walk. As he walked, he saw a bush. The bush was on fire. Moses went to see the burning bush.

. . . God called unto him out of the midst of the bush, and said, Moses, Moses! And he said, Here am I.   *Exodus 3:4*

God spoke to Moses from the bush. God said, "Moses, Moses... I am the God of your father, and the God of Abraham, Isaac, and Jacob." God told Moses He had a special job for him to do.

God Sends Plagues

And the Lord spake unto Moses, Go unto Pharaoh, and say unto him, Thus saith the Lord, Let my people go, that they may serve me.   *Exodus 8:1*

God told Moses to go talk to Pharaoh, and say, "God says, let my people go." Moses obeyed God. Moses told Pharaoh to let the Israelite slaves go free. Pharaoh was not afraid of God or Moses.

And the Lord said unto Moses, Go in unto Pharaoh: for I have hardened his heart . . .
that I might show these my signs before him . . . . *Exodus 10:1*

Pharaoh would not let the slaves go free. God made many bad things happen to Pharaoh and to Egypt. Pharaoh was afraid of God now. Pharaoh let the Israelite slaves go free.

God Frees the Slaves

And it came to pass, when Pharaoh had let the people go . . . God led the people about, through the way of the wilderness of the Red sea . . . .   *Exodus 13:17-18*

God had set His people free from Pharaoh. Moses told the people to get ready for a trip. God was going to lead His people to their very own land. A very special land.

And Moses said unto the people, Remember this day . . . ye came out from Egypt, out of the house of bondage . . . the Lord brought you out from this place . . . . Exodus 13:3

So all of God's people got ready for the big trip. When everything was packed, Moses told the people to follow him. The people were finally going to leave Egypt, once and for all.

Israelites Follow God

And the Lord went before them by day in a pillar of a cloud, to lead them the way . . . and by night in a pillar of fire, to give them light; to go by . . . .   *Exodus 13:21*

God helped His people on their big trip. God made a great big cloud for them to follow. Moses and the people could see the cloud during the day. God loved His people very much.

He took not away the pillar of the cloud by day, nor the pillar of fire by night, from before the people.   *Exodus 13:22*

And at night, God made a great big fire in the sky for His people to follow. The Israelites knew that God was helping them, both day and night. Now Moses and God's people will not get lost.

Walking through a Sea

And Moses said unto the people, Fear ye not, stand still, and see the salvation of the Lord, which he will shew to you today . . . .   *Exodus 14:13*

Pharaoh and his army decided to chase God's people. He wanted to make them slaves again. Moses told the people not to be afraid. He told them, "God will help us escape the Egyptians."

And Moses stretched out his hand over the sea; and the Lord caused the sea to go back . . . and made the sea dry land, and the waters were divided. *Exodus 14:21*

There was one problem. God had led His people to the Red Sea. There was nowhere to go. Then God made a road in the sea. Moses led God's people through the sea. God saved His people.

God Sends Manna

Then said the Lord . . . I will rain bread from heaven for you; and the people shall go out and gather a certain rate every day, that I may prove them . . . .   Exodus 16:4

The people were hungry. They had been walking for a very long time. "We want food," they said. God told Moses that He would feed His people in a very special way.

Then God made it rain. This rain was not made out of water. God made it rain something very special. The rain was made out of bread. God made the sky rain bread, to feed His people.

God Gives Rules

And ye shall be unto me a kingdom of priests, and an holy nation. These are the words which thou shalt speak unto the children of Israel.   *Exodus 19:6*

God led His people to a mountain. God lived on top of the mountain. God told Moses to come up and talk to Him. So Moses went up to the top of the mountain, to visit God.

And Moses said unto the people, Fear not: for God is come to prove you, and that his fear may be before your faces, that ye sin not. Exodus 20:20

God gave Moses ten rules for the people to obey. God wrote the rules down, for Moses, on two stones. God told Moses to teach the new rules to His people. Moses obeyed God.

Israelites Worship a Calf

. . . When the people saw that Moses delayed to come down out of the mount . . . the people . . . said . . . make us gods, which shall go before us . . . .   Exodus 32:1

The people did not know why it was taking Moses so long to come back. The people thought something bad had happened to Moses. They decided to pick a new leader and a new God.

. . . As soon as he came nigh unto the camp, that he saw the calf, and the dancing: and Moses' anger waxed hot . . . he took the calf . . . and burnt it . . . .   Exodus 32:19-20

When Moses came back down the mountain, he saw the people singing and dancing to their new god, a golden calf. Moses told the people to stop worshiping the calf, and to worship God.

People Give Gifts

Take ye from among you an offering unto the Lord: whosoever is of a willing heart, let him bring it . . . gold, and silver, and brass . . . .   Exodus 35:5

The people listened to Moses. They obeyed God's new rules. Moses told the people to show God how much they loved Him. Moses told the people to give God some presents.

The children of Israel brought a willing offering unto the Lord, every man and woman, whose heart made them willing to bring for all manner of work . . . .   Exodus 35:29

So the people who really loved God brought Him many gifts. Some gifts were big, and some were small. God was very happy the people gave Him the gifts.

A House for God

. . . And they brought the Lord's offering to the work of the tabernacle of the congregation, and for all his service, and for the holy garments. Exodus 35:21

Moses used all of the gifts that the people had given to build God a new house. The Israelites were excited. "God is going to live with us," they said. "God is our friend."

When they went into the tent . . . and . . . came near unto the altar . . . then a cloud covered the tent . . . and the glory of the Lord filled the tabernacle. Exodus 40:32-34

The people worked very hard. The people were finished building God's house. They had made a beautiful tent for God to live in. Moses went inside of the tent. God lived inside the new tent.

God Sends Meat

And there went forth a wind from the Lord, and brought quails from the sea, and let them fall by the camp . . . two cubits high . . . .   *Numbers 11:31*

God's people were hungry. "We are tired of eating just bread. We want something new to eat," they said. So Moses asked God what he should do. God told Moses He would feed the people.

. . . The people stood up all that day, and all that night, and all the next day . . . they gathered the quails: and they spread them . . . round about the camp. Numbers 11:32

God made a big wind blow. The big wind made many birds fall to the ground. The birds were called quail. God's people ate the birds. God fed His people again. God was good to the people.

A Good Place to Live

. . . The Lord spake unto Moses, saying, Send thou men, that they may search the land of Canaan, which I give unto the children of Israel . . . .   Numbers 13:1-2

God told Moses to send some men into a land called Canaan. Moses told the men to spy on the people that lived there. "See if they are strong or weak, then come back and tell me," said Moses.

And they told him, and said, We came unto the land whither thou sentest us, and surely it floweth with milk and honey; and this is the fruit of it. *Numbers 13:27*

When the spies returned, they told Moses that the land was good. And that it was filled with good food to eat. "The people are stronger than us," said some of the spies. But Moses was not afraid.

Walls Fall Down

And the Lord said unto Joshua, See, I have given into thine hand Jericho, and the king thereof . . . and you shall compass the city . . . .   *Joshua 6:2-3*

Joshua was the Israelites' new leader. Joshua led God's people into the land of Canaan. There was a city in Canaan called Jericho. God told Joshua to go and capture the city of Jericho.

So the people shouted when the priests blew with the trumpets . . . the wall fell down flat . . . and they took the city.   *Joshua 6:20*

Jericho had great big walls. Joshua and his army did what God told them to do. They marched around the city for seven days. Then they blew trumpets and shouted. Jericho's walls fell down.

Gideon Trusts God

And it came to pass the same night, that the Lord said unto him, Arise, get thee down unto the host; for I have delivered it into thine hand. Judges 7:9

Do you see Gideon? Gideon is an Israelite. God spoke to Gideon and told him to go and capture some bad men. Do you see Gideon's army? God told Gideon to take only three hundred men.

And they stood every man in his place round about the camp: and all the host ran, and cried, and fled . . . three hundred blew the trumpets . . . . Judges 7:21-22

So Gideon's little army blew their trumpets and held up some lamps of fire. It was dark out and the bad men were afraid of the noise and the fire. The bad men ran away as fast as they could run.

God Helps Samson

And the woman bare a son, and called his name Samson: and the child grew, and the Lord blessed him . . . the spirit of the Lord began to move him . . . .   Judges 13:24-25

Samson was one of God's people, also. God told Samson never to cut his hair. God told Samson if he would follow this special rule, God would make Samson very strong. Samson obeyed God.

Then went Samson down . . . to Timnath . . . and behold, a young lion roared against him . . . and he rent him . . . and he had nothing in his hand . . . .   Judges 14:5-6

One day Samson was attacked by a lion. Samson was not afraid. Samson knew God had made him strong. So Samson had a fight with the lion. And Samson won the fight. God helped Samson.

Samuel Wakes Up

The Lord called Samuel: and he answered, Here am I. And he ran unto Eli, and said, Here am I; for thou calledst me.   *1 Samuel 3:4-5*

Samuel was one of God's people. Samuel was a little boy. One night, God called Samuel. Samuel woke up, because he heard someone calling his name. Samuel did not know it was God calling.

And the Lord said to Samuel . . . I will do a thing in Israel, at which both the ears of everyone that heareth it shall tingle.   *1 Samuel 3:11*

God called Samuel's name once more. This time Samuel knew it was God. God told Samuel, "I am going to do something special for My people." Samuel believed God. God loved Samuel.

Saul Is King

. . . Samuel took a vial of oil, and poured it upon his head . . . and said, is it not because the Lord hath anointed thee to be captain over his inheritance?   *1 Samuel 10:1*

When little Samuel was older, he met a man named Saul. Samuel knew that Saul was going to be the Israelites, new king. God told Samuel to pour oil on Saul's head. Samuel obeyed God.

And the spirit of the Lord will come upon thee, and thou shalt prophesy with them, and shalt be turned into another man.   *1 Samuel 10:6*

God saw Samuel pour the special oil on Saul's head. God helped Saul to become the new king. God's people were very happy. They had a new king. Saul was happy, too.

David Fights Goliath

And David said to Saul, Let no man's heart fail because of him; thy servant will go and fight with this Philistine.   *1 Samuel 17:32*

One day King Saul had a big problem. A giant named Goliath was going to hurt God's people. The giant said, "Send someone out to fight me." Everyone was afraid to fight the giant.

So David prevailed over the Philistine with a sling and with a stone, and smote the Philistine, and slew him . . . .   *1 Samuel 17:50*

A young shepherd boy came to King Saul, and said, "I am not afraid of this giant." David ran out to meet the giant. He took his sling and killed the giant. David knew that God had helped him.

David and Jonathan

. . . Jonathan . . . delighted much in David: and Jonathan told David . . . Saul my father seeketh to kill thee . . . what I see, that I will tell thee.   *1 Samuel 19:2-3*

After David killed the big giant, the Israelites liked David more than King Saul. They wanted David to be their king. This made King Saul very mad. Jonathan was King Saul's son.

And Jonathan spake good of David unto Saul his father, and said . . . Let not the king sin against his servant, against David . . . .   1 Samuel 19:4

Jonathan told David, "My father is going to hurt you, quick run away from here." Jonathan was David's friend. Jonathan loved David. David ran away from King Saul so he would not hurt him.

God's Wonderful House

. . . I purpose to build an house unto the name of the Lord my God, as the Lord spake . . . he shall build an house unto my name.   *1 Kings 5:5*

When David was older he became the king. David loved God and promised to build God a new house. David had a son. Solomon was David's son. Solomon loved God, too.

So he built the house, and finished it; and covered the house with beams and boards of cedar. And the word of the Lord came to Solomon.   *1 Kings 6:9-11*

Solomon built God a beautiful new house. It was the most beautiful house in all of the world. God liked the new house that Solomon built. God loved Solomon very much.

Birds Feed Elijah

And it shall be, that thou shalt drink of the brook; and I have commanded the ravens to feed thee there.　　　　　　　　　　　　　　　　　　　　　*1 Kings 17:4*

Elijah loved God. Elijah would tell the people about God. God told Elijah to go and live by a brook. Elijah was hungry and there was nothing to eat. God knew Elijah was hungry.

And the ravens brought him bread and flesh in the morning, and bread and flesh in the evening; and he drank of the brook.   *1 Kings 17:6*

God sent some birds to feed Elijah. The birds would bring Elijah bread and meat each morning and each night. God loved Elijah. That's why God took care of him.

God Gives Food

And Elijah said . . . Fear not; go and . . . make thereof a little cake first, and bring it unto me, and after make for thee and for thy son.   *1 Kings 17:13*

God told Elijah to go and visit a woman. Elijah obeyed God. When Elijah got to the woman's house he said, "Please get me a drink of water and some bread." The woman was sad.

And she went and did according to the saying of Elijah: and she, and he, and her house, did eat many days. 1 Kings 17:15

The woman did not have enough food to feed Elijah. Elijah told the woman not to be afraid. Elijah knew that God would feed them. Elijah was right. God made extra food for everyone.

God Shows His Power

And call ye on the name of your gods, and I will call on the name of the Lord: and the God that answereth by fire, let him be God . . . .   *1 Kings 18:24*

There were some bad people who did not love God. They told Elijah that his God was not as strong as their god. Elijah did not believe them. Elijah knew that his God was stronger.

Then the fire of the Lord fell, and consumed the burnt-sacrifice . . . when all the people saw it . . . they said, The Lord, he is the God; the Lord, he is the God.

1 Kings 18:38-39

Elijah told the bad men that his God would do something special, and God did! Elijah poured water on some wood. Elijah called out to God, and God burned the wet wood. Elijah was right.

People Welcome Elisha

And she said unto her husband, Behold now, I perceive that this is an holy man of God, which passeth by us continually.   *2 Kings 4:9*

Do you see Elisha? He has made some new friends. This woman and her husband like Elisha. They know that Elisha loves God. Elisha needs a place to eat and sleep.

Let us make a little chamber . . . and let us set for him there a bed, and a table, and a stool, and a candlestick . . . .   2 Kings 4:10

Elisha's new friends gave Elisha his own room. They gave him a bed, a table, a stool, and a candlestick. They showed Elisha that they loved him. They helped Elisha.

Nehemiah's Plan

. . . The wall of Jerusalem also is broken down, and the gates thereof are burned with fire . . . when I heard these words, . . . I sat down and wept.   *Nehemiah 1:3-4*

Nehemiah loved God. Many of God's people lived in a city called Jerusalem. Nehemiah loved Jerusalem, too. Nehemiah is sad because the walls of Jerusalem are broken.

Now it came to pass, when the wall was built . . . I gave my brother Hanani, and Hananiah . . . charge over Jerusalem . . . .   *Nehemiah 7:1-2*

Nehemiah told God's people, "We should fix these broken walls." God's people agreed with Nehemiah. Nehemiah and the people of Jerusalem fixed the broken walls!

Esther Saves Her People

And the king said again unto Esther . . . What is thy petition, queen Esther? and it shall be granted thee: and what is thy request?   *Esther 7:2*

Esther was the new queen. The king of Persia did not know Esther was a Jew. A man named Haman did not like the Jews because they would not bow down to him. Haman was angry.

And Esther said, The adversary and enemy is this wicked Haman. Then Haman was afraid before the king and queen.   *Esther 7:6*

Haman asked the king if he could hurt the Jews. The king said, "Yes." Then Esther told the king that she was also a Jew and that Haman was a bad man. The king decided not to hurt the Jews.

Job Trusts God

There was a man in the land of Uz, whose name was Job; and that man was perfect and upright, and one that feared God and eschewed evil.   Job 1:1

Job was very sad. Many bad things happened to Job. Job loved God very much. God loved Job, also. Job lost his family and many other things. Job's friends told him God was mad at him.

So the Lord blessed the latter end of Job more than his beginning . . . he had fourteen thousand sheep . . . seven sons . . . and three daughters. Job 42:12-13

But God was not mad at Job. God was teaching Job how to trust Him. Even when everything was very bad, Job still loved and trusted God. God blessed Job and gave him a new family.

God Protects Daniel

Then the king commanded, and they brought Daniel, and cast him into the den of lions . . . the king spake . . . unto Daniel . . . Thy God . . . will deliver thee.   Daniel 6:16

Daniel is in a lot of trouble. Do you see the lions? Daniel would not stop praying to God, so the king put Daniel in the lions' den. It was against the king's law to pray to anyone except the king.

My God hath sent his angel, and hath shut the lions' mouths . . . So Daniel was taken up out of the den . . . because he believed in his God.   Daniel 6:22-23

God helped Daniel. God told the lions not to hurt Daniel. The lions obeyed God. Daniel was safe. The king loved Daniel and decided to change the law. Now everyone could pray to Daniel's God.

A Fish Swallows Jonah

Now the Lord had prepared a great fish to swallow up Jonah. And Jonah was in the belly of the fish three days and three nights.   *Jonah 1:17*

Jonah was an Israelite. God told Jonah to go tell some people about God. Jonah was afraid to tell the people about God. He thought that they might hurt him. So Jonah got on a boat.

And the Lord spake unto the fish, and it vomited out Jonah upon the dry land . . . Jonah arose, and went unto Nineveh, according to the word of the Lord . . . . Jonah 2:10; 3:3

Jonah tried to run away. God sent a big storm. Jonah said, "Throw me into the water, and the storm will stop." God sent a big fish to swallow Jonah and save him. Then Jonah obeyed God.

An Angel Appears

And the angel came in unto her, and said, Hail, thou that art highly favored, the Lord is with thee: blessed art thou among women . . . Fear not Mary . . . .   Luke 1:28-30

An angel came to see Mary. The angel was sent from God. The angel told Mary that something very special was going to happen. The angel told Mary that she was going to have a baby boy.

And behold, thou shalt conceive in thy womb, and bring forth a son, and shalt call his name JESUS . . . and of his kingdom there shall be no end.   Luke 1:31-33

The angel told Mary to name the baby Jesus. The angel also said that this baby was God's very own Son. Mary was very happy. Mary loved God very much. God loved Mary, too.

Baby Jesus Is Born

For unto you is born this day in the city of David a Saviour, which is Christ the Lord.
Luke 2:11

Baby Jesus is God's Son. Do you see Mary? Do you see Joseph? They are taking care of baby Jesus. Everything that the angel told Mary was true.

And this shall be a sign unto you; Ye shall find the babe wrapped in swaddling clothes, lying in a manger. *Luke 2:12*

Baby Jesus was born in Bethlehem. He is lying in a manger. The animals are watching baby Jesus. Do you see baby Jesus? He really is God's Son!

Shepherds Worship Jesus

And there were in the same country shepherds abiding in the field, keeping watch over their flock by night. And lo, the angel of the Lord came upon them . . . .   *Luke 2:8-9*

An angel told some shepherds about baby Jesus. The shepherds wanted to go see God's Son. The angel told the shepherds just where they could find baby Jesus.

. . . The shepherds said . . . Let us now go even unto Bethlehem . . . And they came with haste, and found Mary, and Joseph, and the babe lying in a manger. Luke 2:15-16

The angel told the shepherds that they would find baby Jesus asleep in a manger. "There's the baby," they said. "There is God's Son." The shepherds were glad they found baby Jesus.

Wise Men Bring Gifts

When they had heard the king, they departed . . . the star, which they saw in the east, went before them, till it . . . stood over where the young child was. *Matthew 2:9*

Do you see the wise men? They are also looking for God's Son. They want to give baby Jesus some special presents. God put a bright, shiny star in the sky for the wise men to follow.

. . . When they were come into the house, they saw the . . . child...fell down, and worshipped him . . . they presented him gifts; gold . . . frankincense, and myrrh.

Matthew 2:11

The wise men followed the bright star for many days. "Look, over there, that is where we will find God's Son," said the wise men. Off they went to give baby Jesus His presents.

Jesus' Family Escapes

. . . The angel of the Lord appeareth to Joseph in a dream, saying, Arise, and take the young child and his mother, and flee into Egypt . . . .   *Matthew 2:13*

Herod was the king. King Herod was a bad man. Herod heard that baby Jesus was going to be king someday, and this made him very angry. Herod wanted to hurt baby Jesus.

When he arose, he took the young child and his mother by night, and departed into Egypt: and was there until the death of Herod . . . .   *Matthew 2:14-15*

An angel told Joseph to take baby Jesus to Egypt. King Herod could not hurt baby Jesus there. So Joseph took Mary and baby Jesus to Egypt. God had helped Jesus and His family.

Jesus Grows

And the child grew, and waxed strong in spirit, filled with wisdom; and the grace of God was upon him.   *Luke 2:40*

Jesus was growing up. Jesus was not a baby anymore, He was a young boy. Jesus went to the temple with His mom and dad. Jesus was very smart. Everyone knew that Jesus was special.

And Joseph and his mother marvelled at those things which were spoken of him . . . his parents went to Jerusalem every year at the feast of the passover.   *Luke 2:33-41*

Joseph was a carpenter. He took care of Mary and Jesus. Mary and Joseph liked it when people told them nice things about Jesus. Mary, Joseph, and Jesus are getting ready to go on a special trip.

Grown-ups Listen

And when he was twelve years old, they went up to Jerusalem after the custom of the feast . . . as they returned, the child Jesus tarried behind . . . .   *Luke 2:42-43*

When Jesus was twelve years old, He went on a special trip with His mom and dad. They went to Jerusalem to celebrate Passover. Mary and Joseph did not know where Jesus was.

. . . After three days they found him in the temple, sitting in the midst of the doctors, both hearing them, and asking them questions. *Luke 2:46*

Jesus wanted to talk about God. So Jesus went to talk with the teachers. They were amazed at how smart young Jesus was. Mary and Joseph found Jesus, They were happy, too.

John the Baptist

And John was clothed with camel's hair, and with a girdle of a skin about his loins; and he did eat locusts and wild honey.

Mark 1:6

Do you see John? This is John the Baptist. He was sent by God to tell people to get ready for Jesus. John wore very funny clothes and ate bugs and honey.

And he preached, saying, . . . I indeed have baptized you with water: but he shall bap-
tize you with the Holy Ghost.   *Mark 2:7-8*

John told the people to be baptized in the water to show their love for God. The people obeyed John and were baptized in the water. John told them that God's Son was coming to talk to them.

Jesus Is Baptized

. . . Jesus . . . was baptized of John in Jordan . . . and coming straightway up out of the water, he saw the heavens opened . . . and the Spirit like a dove descending upon him.
Mark 1:9-10

One day Jesus came to talk to the people, just like John had said. But first, "I, too, must be baptized," said Jesus. John told Jesus that He did not have to be baptized, like the others.

And there came a voice from heaven, saying, Thou art my beloved Son, in whom I am well pleased.   *Mark 1:11*

Jesus told John to baptize Him. John obeyed Jesus. John baptized Jesus. Suddenly a dove came down from heaven and landed on Jesus. Then God spoke, and said, "I am well pleased."

Satan Tempts Jesus

Then was Jesus led up of the Spirit . . . to be tempted of the devil . . . And when he had fasted forty days and forty nights, he was . . . hungered. Matthew 4:1-2

Jesus went into the desert. Jesus was very tired and hungry. Satan was very bad, and he tried to trick Jesus. Satan knew that Jesus was tired and hungry. Satan wanted Jesus to disobey God.

And when the tempter came to him, he said, If thou be the Son of God, command that these stones be made bread.   *Matthew 4:3*

He told Jesus to do some bad things. Jesus did not do the bad things. Jesus wanted to obey God. Jesus loved God very much. Jesus knew that if He obeyed God that God would take care of Him.

Nicodemus Asks Questions

There was a man . . . named Nicodemus . . . The same came to Jesus by night, and said unto him, Rabbi, we know that thou art a teacher come from God . . . .   *John 3:1-2*

Nicodemus did not want anyone to see him talking to Jesus. So he came to see Jesus in the night. He wanted to ask Jesus some questions about God.

Jesus answered and said unto him, Verily, verily, I say unto thee, Except a man be born again, he cannot see the kingdom of God. *John 3:3*

Jesus told Nicodemus about God. Jesus told Nicodemus that if he wanted to go to heaven, he should start his life over again. And this time he must trust God to help him be good.

A Woman Is Forgiven

There cometh a woman of Samaria to draw water: Jesus saith unto her, Give me to drink.   *John 4:7*

One day Jesus went for a walk. Jesus stopped to rest near a well. Jesus met a woman there at the well. Jesus talked to the woman. Jesus asked the woman to get Him a drink of water.

The woman then left her waterpot, and went . . . into the city . . . Come, see a man, which told me all things that I ever did: is not this the Christ?   *John 4:28-29*

Jesus knew many secrets about the woman, and some of them were bad. But Jesus loved the woman anyway. The woman went and told many of her friends about Jesus and His special love.

Jesus Helps His Friends

. . . Master, we have toiled all the night, and have taken nothing: nevertheless, at thy word I will let down the net.   Luke 5:5

Peter and his friends went fishing. They fished all night long and still did not catch any fish. Jesus loved Peter and his friends. Jesus wanted to help them catch some fish.

And when they had this done, they inclosed a great multitude of fishes: and their net brake . . . Fear not; from henceforth thou shalt catch men . . . .   Luke 5:6-10

Jesus told His friends to let down their net into the water one more time. They obeyed Jesus. When Peter and his friends pulled their net back into the boat, it was filled with fish.

Jesus Says, "Follow Me!"

And Jesus . . . saw two brethren, Simon called Peter, and Andrew his brother, casting a net into the sea; for they were fishers.   Matthew 4:18

After Jesus helped His friends catch all of the fish, Jesus said something very special to them. Jesus told them to follow Him instead of being fishermen. Jesus wanted to be their teacher.

And he saith unto them, Follow me, and I will make you fishers of men . . . And they straightway left their nets, and followed him.
Matthew 4:19-20

So Peter and Andrew obeyed Jesus and laid down their fishing nets. Then Peter and Andrew followed Jesus everywhere He went. Jesus taught His friends about God's love for them.

A Sick Man

And they come unto him, bringing one sick of the palsy . . . they uncovered the roof where he was . . . they let down the bed . . . . Mark 2:3-4

Wherever Jesus went many people would come and listen to Him talk. Some people believed that Jesus was God's Son. They brought a very sick man to Jesus. They could not get in the house.

When Jesus saw their faith, he said unto the sick of the palsy, Son, thy sins be forgiven thee . . . Arise, and take up thy bed . . . he arose . . . .   Mark 2:5-12

So they lowered the sick man down through the roof of the house. Jesus knew they believed He was God's Son. Jesus healed the sick man, and he was not sick anymore. The people were happy.

The Twelve Disciples

And he goeth up into a mountain, and calleth unto him whom he would: and they came unto him.
Mark 3:13

Many people liked to follow Jesus. They liked to watch all of the sick people get better. And they liked it when Jesus would talk to them. Jesus was looking for twelve very special helpers.

And he ordained twelve, that they should be with him, and that he might send them forth to preach . . . and to . . . heal . . . .   *Mark 3:14-15*

He wanted the twelve helpers to talk about God's love and help other sick people, just like Jesus did. Look, Jesus found His special helpers. Would you like to be one of Jesus' special helpers, too?

How to Be Good

And seeing the multitudes, he went up into a mountain . . . and he opened his mouth and he taught them . . . .
Matthew 5:1-2

Sometimes when Jesus would talk to the people, He would climb up the side of a hill. That way everyone could see and hear Him. Jesus would tell the people how to be good.

Blessed are they which do hunger and thirst after righteousness: for they shall be filled . . . Blessed are the merciful, for they shall obtain mercy . . . .   Matthew 5:6-7

Jesus told the people how much God loved them. Jesus also told the people that they should show each other God's love. Jesus told the people that God would always take care of them.

A Boy Lives Again

. . . There was a dead man carried out, the only son of his mother, she was a widow . . . and when the Lord saw her, he had compassion on her . . . . Luke 7:12-13

Jesus could make sick people get well. This boy was so sick that he died. The people did not know that Jesus could even help someone who had died. Jesus stopped and touched the boy.

And he came and touched the bier . . . And he said. Young man, I say unto thee, Arise . . . And he that was dead sat up, and began to speak . . . . Luke 7:14-15

When Jesus touched him, the boy sat up and began to talk. Jesus helped the dead boy come back to life again. The boy's mother was so happy. She knew that Jesus really was God's Son.

Jesus Tells Stories

And great multitudes were gathered unto him, so that he went into a ship, and sat; and the whole multitude stood on the shore.   *Matthew 13:2*

One day, there were too many people following Jesus. Jesus wanted everyone to be able to hear about God's love. So He got into a boat and went out on the water. Everyone could see Jesus now.

And he spake many things unto them in parables, saying . . . Who hath ears to hear, let him hear . . . .   *Matthew 13:3-9*

Jesus began to tell the people stories. Jesus knew that the people would listen to His stories. And the people did. Jesus told the people to listen very carefully because His stories were true.

Jesus Calms a Storm

And there arose a great storm of wind, and the waves beat into the ship, so that it was now full . . . and they awake him . . . .   Mark 4:37-38

Sometimes Jesus would travel from city to city in a boat. One day a terrible storm came. The storm shook the boat that Jesus was in. Jesus was sleeping when the storm came.

And he arose, and rebuked the wind, and said unto the sea, Peace be still. And the wind ceased, and there was a great calm . . . .   Mark 4:39

Other people on the boat were afraid of the big storm. They thought that the boat might sink. They asked Jesus to help them, and He did. Jesus told the big storm to go away, and it did.

A Girl Lives Again

And he put them all out, and took her by the hand, and called, saying, Maid, arise.
Luke 8:54

This little girl had died. Her father was very sad. Jesus came to see the dead girl. He told her to get up and she did. She was alive again!

And her spirit came again, and she arose straightway: and he commanded to give her meat. And her parents were astonished . . . .   Luke 81:55,56

The little girl's father wasn't sad anymore. He was happy, because Jesus made his daughter come back to life again. The little girl was happy, too.

Jesus Feeds 5,000 People

There is a lad here, which hath five barley loaves, and two small fishes: but what are they among so many?
John 6:9

Sometimes, when people would come to hear Jesus talk, they would not have enough food to eat. These people got very hungry. Jesus knew that the people were hungry.

And Jesus took the loaves; and when he had given thanks, he distributed to the disciples, and the disciples, to them . . . that were set down . . . they were filled . . . .

John 6:11-12

A boy came to Jesus and said, "I will share my lunch with the hungry people." So Jesus took the little boy's lunch and turned it into 5,000 lunches. Jesus gave everyone that was hungry some food.

Jesus Walks on the Sea

And when Peter was come down out of the ship . . . he was afraid; and beginning to sink, he cried, saying, Lord, save me.   Matthew 14:29-30

Peter and some of his friends were in a boat. Jesus did not go in the boat with them. Jesus wanted to go to the other side of the lake. So, He walked right on top of the water.

And immediately Jesus stretched forth his hand, and caught him, and said unto him, O thou of little faith, wherefore didst thou doubt? Matthew 14:31

Peter saw Jesus walking on top of the water. Peter wanted to walk on top of the water, too. When Peter stepped out on the water he began to sink. Jesus saw Peter sinking and helped him.

Jesus Takes Care of Us

And when he putteth forth his own sheep, he goeth before them, and the sheep follow him: for they know his voice.   John 10:4

Do you see the shepherd? He loves his sheep very much. The shepherd takes very good care of his sheep. He feeds them and helps them when they get lost.

I am the good shepherd, and know my sheep, and am known of mine . . . and I lay down my life for the sheep . . . .   John 10:14-15

Jesus is your shepherd. Jesus loves you very much. Jesus will take very good care of you, too. Jesus wants to take care of you just like the shepherd takes care of his sheep.

Mary and Martha

. . . He entered into a certain village: and a certain woman, named Martha, received him into her house . . . And she had a sister called Mary . . . .   Luke 10:38-39

Jesus liked to go to people's houses to visit them. One day Jesus visited Mary and Martha. Mary sat and listened to each and every story that Jesus told. Martha was too busy to listen.

And Jesus answered, and said unto her, Martha, Martha . . . Mary hath chosen the good part, which shall not be taken away from her.   *Luke 10:41-42*

Jesus told Martha not to be so busy. He told her to listen and learn about God's love. Mary liked to hear about God's love. Martha was thinking about other things instead.

A Lost Sheep

What man of you having an hundred sheep, if he lose one of them, doth not leave the ninety and nine . . . and go after that which is lost until he find it? . . . .   Luke 15:4

Jesus told the people another story. This story was about a shepherd who lost one of his sheep. The shepherd had many other sheep, but he wanted to find the one sheep that was lost.

And when he hath found it, he layeth it on his shoulders, rejoicing . . . I have found my sheep which was lost . . . .   Luke 15: 5-6

The shepherd looked for the little lost sheep. Look, the shepherd found his lost sheep. The shepherd is very happy. He loves his sheep very much. Jesus loves you very much, too.

A Son Comes Home

. . . Not many days after, the younger son gathered all together, and took his journey into a far country, and . . . wasted his substance with riotous living.   *Luke 15:13*

There was a boy who did not want to live at home anymore. He wanted to move far away. So the boy asked his father for some money and off he went. The boy moved to another land.

And the son said unto him, Father, I have sinned against heaven, and in thy sight, and am no more worthy to be called thy son. *Luke 15:21*

The boy spent the money on bad things. When the boy ran out of money, he wanted to go back home. The boy was sorry for what he had done. The boy's father was happy to see his son again.

Lazarus Lives Again

. . . And after that he saith unto them, Our friend Lazarus sleepeth; but I go that I may awake him out of sleep.   *John 11:11*

Mary and Martha had a brother named Lazarus. Lazarus was very sick. One day Lazarus was so sick that he died. Mary and Martha were very sad. They missed their brother very much.

And when he had thus spoken, he cried with a loud voice, Lazarus, come forth. And he that was dead came forth . . . .   *John 11:43-44*

When they told Jesus what had happened to Lazarus, Jesus was sad, too. Then Jesus told Lazarus, "Come back to life," and Lazarus did. Everyone was happy because Lazarus was alive.

155

Ten Men Are Sick

And as he entered a certain village, there met him ten men that were lepers . . . and said, Jesus, Master, have mercy on us.   *Luke 17:12-13*

Jesus met ten men who were very sick. These men were going to die. The ten sick men asked Jesus to heal them. They did not want to be sick. Jesus healed all ten of the sick men.

And Jesus answering said, Were there not ten cleansed? but where are the nine? . . .
Arise, go thy way: thy faith hath made thee whole.   Luke 17:17-19

Only one of the men came back to thank Jesus for making him well. Jesus asked him about the other nine men and why they didn't come back to say thank you. Jesus wants us to be thankful.

Jesus Loves All Children

And they brought young children to him, that he should touch them; and his disciples rebuked those that brought them.   *Mark 10:13*

Some children came to see Jesus. The children liked Jesus because He was kind to them. The big people told the children to leave Jesus alone. But Jesus wanted the children to be near Him.

. . .Whosoever shall not receive the kingdom of God as a little child, he shall not enter therein . . . And he took them up into his arms . . . .   Mark 10:15-16

Jesus loves children very much. Jesus loves you very much, too. Jesus knows that children want to spend time with Him. Jesus wants to spend some time with you.

Jesus Helps a Blind Man

. . . Blind Bartimaeus . . . began to cry out, and say, Jesus, thou son of David, have mercy on me.   *Mark 10:46-47*

Do you see Bartimaeus? Bartimaeus cannot see. Bartimaeus is blind. Bartimaeus did not like being blind. He wanted to see like everyone else. Bartimaeus asked Jesus to help him see again.

And Jesus answered . . . What wilt thou that I should do unto thee? . . . the blind man said . . . I might receive my sight . . . immediately he received his sight . . . .

Mark 10:51-52

Jesus loved Bartimaeus. Jesus helped Bartimaeus. He wasn't blind anymore. Now Bartimaeus really knew that Jesus was God's Son. Bartimaeus loved Jesus because Jesus had helped him.

Zacchaeus Climbs a Tree

And Jesus entered . . . Jericho . . . a man named Zacchaeus . . . sought to see Jesus . . . and could not . . . because he was little of stature . . . .　　　　*Luke 19:1-3*

Zacchaeus was a little man. He could not see past the other people in front of him. He was too little. When Zacchaeus heard that Jesus was coming, he had an idea.

Zacchaeus . . . climbed up into a sycamore-tree . . . Jesus . . . said unto him, Zacchaeus . . . come down: for today I must abide at thy house.   Luke 19:2-5

Zacchaeus climbed up in a sycamore tree so he could see Jesus. When Jesus saw Zacchaeus up in the tree, He said, "Zacchaeus, I want to come and visit you today." Zacchaeus was happy.

People Wave Palms

And the disciples . . . brought the . . . colt, and put on them their clothes, and they set him thereon.   Matthew 21:6-7

Everywhere that Jesus went, people were very glad to see Him. The people wanted to make Jesus their king. The people would lay palm branches on the ground in front of Jesus.

And a very great multitude . . . cut down branches from the trees, and strewed them in the way . . . saying, Hosanna to the Son of David . . . .   *Matthew 21:8-9*

They wanted to let Jesus know how much they liked Him. The people shouted, "Hosanna to the Son of David!" They believed that Jesus was special. Do you believe that Jesus is special?

A Poor Woman's Gift

And there came a certain poor widow, and she threw in two mites, which make a farthing . . . and he called unto him his disciples . . . .   Mark 12:42-43

This woman is putting money in a box. The money is to help take care of the church. This woman does not have a lot of money. But she wants to help the church.

. . . And saith unto them . . . this poor widow hath cast more in, than all they which have cast into the treasury . . . she . . . cast in all that she had . . . .　　　Mark 12:43-44

Jesus saw the woman put money in the box. Jesus knows that she put in all of the money that she had. The woman knows that God will take care of her. She loves God more than money.

A Special Meal

And he took bread, and gave thanks, and brake it, and gave unto them, saying, This is my body which is broken for you: this do in remembrance of me.   Luke 22:19

Some people did not like Jesus. They wanted to hurt Him. Jesus knew that the bad people would be coming soon. So He asked His twelve special friends to eat one last supper with Him.

Likewise also the cup after supper, saying, This cup is the new testament in my blood, which is shed for you . . . .   Luke 22:20

Jesus told them to remember Him after He was gone. He was trying to tell His friends that He had to go away. Jesus' twelve friends did not really believe that He would go away.

Jesus Prays

And he taketh with him Peter, and James, and John, and began to be sore amazed, and to be very heavy . . . .   *Mark 14:33*

After Jesus and His friends finished eating, He asked them to come and pray with Him. Jesus liked to pray. He liked to talk to God. God was His father. Jesus knelt down and began to pray.

And he went forward a little, and fell on the ground, and prayed that, if it were possible, the hour might pass from him . . . . Mark 14:35

When Jesus stopped praying, He saw that His friends were asleep. He wanted them to stay awake with Him and pray. Jesus knew that some bad men were coming to hurt Him.

Jesus Dies on the Cross

And they spit upon him . . . and after that they had mocked him, they took the robe off from him . . . and led him away . . . they crucified him . . . .   Matthew 27:30-35

When Jesus had stopped praying, the bad men came. They took Jesus away from His special friends. The bad men hurt Jesus. They did not want Jesus to be their new king.

Jesus, when he had cried again with a loud voice, yielded up the ghost . . . many women were there . . . which followed Jesus . . . .
Matthew 27:50-55

They put Jesus on a cross made of wood. Jesus cried with a loud voice. And then He died. Some people were sad because Jesus had been very kind to them. Others were glad that He was dead.

Jesus Is Alive

Now upon the first day of the week . . . they found the stone rolled away . . . and they entered in, and found not the body of the Lord Jesus . . . .   Luke 24:1-3

After Jesus had died, His friends buried Him in a tomb. Three days later Jesus came back to life again. Jesus is alive! When Jesus' friends came to the tomb, they could not find Jesus.

. . . Behold two men stood by them in shining garments . . . He is not here, but is risen . . . and they remembered his words . . . .   Luke 24:4-6

Suddenly two angels appeared and told them that Jesus was really alive. All of Jesus' friends were very happy. They missed Jesus very much. Only God could do such a wonderful thing.

Jesus Returns to Heaven

And when he had spoken these things, while they beheld, he was taken up; and a cloud received him out of their sight.   *Acts 1:9*

After Jesus came back to life, He visited all of His friends. Now they were sure that He was God's Son. Jesus did many wonderful things for His friends. Jesus was glad to see them.

And while they looked steadfastly toward heaven, as he went up, behold, two men stood by them, in white apparel . . . .   *Acts 1:10*

One day Jesus told His friends that He was going to live with God in heaven. Jesus told His friends that when they die they can come and live with Him in heaven, too. Then Jesus went up to heaven.

177

God Sends the Holy Spirit

And when the day of Pentecost was fully come . . . suddenly there came a sound from heaven, as of a rushing mighty wind . . . and it filled the house . . . .   *Acts 2:1-2*

After Jesus had gone back to heaven, His friends were praying together. All of a sudden there was a very loud noise in the sky. Everyone wondered what the noise was.

178

And there appeared unto them cloven tongues like as of fire . . . and they were all filled with the Holy Ghost . . . . Acts 2:3-4

God had sent all of Jesus' friends His Holy Spirit. Jesus had told them that this would happen. The Holy Spirit would help Jesus' friends to pray. The Holy Spirit lived with Jesus' friends.

A Man from Ethiopia

. . . Behold, a man from Ethiopia, a eunuch of great authority . . . had come to Jerusalem for to worship, was returning and sitting in his chariot . . . .   Acts 8:27-28

One day a man was riding down the road. This man had never heard about Jesus. He was from Ethiopia. One of Jesus' friends was walking down the same road.

And Philip ran thither to him, and heard him read the prophet Esaias, and said, Understandest thou what thou readest?   Acts 8:30

"I will tell you about Jesus," said the walking man. He then told the Ethiopian man how Jesus died and came back to life again. The Ethiopian man became one of Jesus' friends, too.

Saul Sees a Great Light

And Saul, yet breathing out threatenings and slaughter against the disciples of the Lord, went unto the high priest.   *Acts 9:1*

There were still many people who did not want to be friends with Jesus. Saul was one of them. Saul loved God, but he did not love Jesus. One day Saul was walking down a road.

And as he journeyed . . . there shined round about him a light from heaven . . . he fell to the earth and heard a voice . . . I am Jesus . . . . Acts 9:3-5

He saw a great light shining down from the sky. The light hurt his eyes. Then he heard a voice say, "Saul, I am Jesus." Saul had finally met Jesus and wanted to be His friend, too.

Barnabas Helps Saul

But Barnabas took him, and brought him to the apostles, and declared unto them how he had seen the Lord in the way . . . . Acts 9:27

Many of Jesus' friends were afraid of Saul. They did not know that Saul had met Jesus. They did not know that Saul loved Jesus. A man named Barnabas found out about Saul.

And he was with them coming in and going out at Jerusalem . . . And he spake boldly in the name of the Lord Jesus . . . . Acts 9:28-29

Barnabas told everyone that Saul was like them now. Barnabas told them that Saul loved Jesus very much. Saul was glad that Barnabas helped him. Saul loved Barnabas, too.

Dorcas Lives Again

Now there was at Joppa a certain disciple named . . . Dorcas; this woman was full of good works and alms-deeds that she did.   Acts 9:36

There was a woman from Joppa whose name was Dorcas. Dorcas loved Jesus. Everyone loved Dorcas because she was so kind. One day Dorcas got very sick and died. Everyone was sad.

And it came to pass in those days, that she was sick, and died . . . But Peter prayed . . . And she opened her eyes . . . she sat up . . . .   Acts 9:40

Peter came to visit Dorcas. Some people thought Peter was too late. But Peter knew that God would help Dorcas. So Peter prayed to God and Dorcas came back to life again.

Paul and Silas

And at midnight Paul and Silas prayed, and sang praises unto God . . . suddenly there was a great earthquake . . . everyone's bands were loosed. Acts 16:25-26

Jesus told Saul to change his name to Paul. Now Paul and his friend Silas were in jail because they had been talking about Jesus too much. But they were not sad at all . . . they were singing!

And the keeper of the prison awaking out of his sleep . . . said, Sirs, what must I do to be saved? Acts 16:27-30

Jesus helped Paul and Silas by making the prison doors come open all by themselves. Jesus had set them free. The man in charge of the jail saw what happened. He wanted to become Jesus' friend, too.

189

Paul Talks to a King

Then Agrippa said unto Paul, Thou art permitted to speak for thyself. Then Paul stretched forth the hand, and answered for himself.   *Acts 26:1*

The king put Paul in jail again for talking too much about Jesus. But Paul did not mind. Paul wanted everyone to become one of Jesus' friends. Paul wanted to tell the king about Jesus.

That Christ should suffer, and that he should be the first that should rise from the dead, and should shew light unto the people . . . .   Acts 26:23

Paul told the king about Jesus. He said, "Jesus is God's Son and He loves you. Only Jesus can help you go to heaven after you die." The king listened to Paul. The king liked Paul.